Liar! Liar!

Lies Told by Imperfect People,
Used by a Perfect God

Ron Klave

CROSSLINK
PUBLISHING

Liar! Liar!: Lies Told by Imperfect People, Used by a Perfect God

CrossLink Publishing
www.crosslink.org

ISBN 978-1-936746-85-9

Library of Congress Control Number: 2013952737

Dedications

To my friends, Marisa Barton and Chad Compton: Your friendship, your love, your sacrifices, and your insight helped me fulfill a dream.

To my Pastor, Arron: When I came to you, you saw more in me than I saw in myself. Your encouragement and friendship are priceless. I love ya, man!

To my Pastor, Patrick: You lift me up, encourage me, challenge me, and inspire me. Most importantly, you love me unconditionally as a brother in Christ and as a dear friend. I love ya, bro!

To my kids, Tori and Isaiah: Your love overwhelms me and melts my heart.

To Wendy, the one my soul loves: I would say "I do" all over again. Without you, this Bible study would have remained only in my mind—unfinished. Your love humbles me. You still take my breath away!

To Jesus Christ, My Lord and my Savior: I have never fully understood why You called a man like me to Your kingdom. I can only hope and pray that the letter You are writing in my life brings honor and glory to You.

Contents

Introduction

Let's be real for a moment! We sometimes lie—and when we do, it is often to protect ourselves without thought or compassion for others, without consideration of the potential consequences and the affect of those consequences on ourselves, our families, and our Savior.

There are consequences of each lie. Some lies have immediate repercussions, while some lies have future consequences. Jesus Christ died for each lie told in our lives, yet we continue to lie without fail.

So did some of God's chosen people lie? Is it okay to lie to protect a loved one? Are all lies sin? Why were some lies seemingly ignored without consequence, and why were some lies punished? Is it even possible to live a godly life without having to tell a lie in a fallen world?

These questions and more are the reasons why I explored each lie told by imperfect people in the book of Genesis, and how God dealt with each lie.

This study can be used for your own personal devotions, or it can be used in a small group setting...or both. The study is designed to do at your own pace, allowing the Lord to speak to you.

My prayer is that you find this study as enriching as I did. I only want to bring honor to God and truth to you.

— Ron Klave

Genesis 3:1

Now the serpent was more crafty than any other beast of the field that the Lord God had made. He said to the woman, "Did God actually say, 'You shall not eat from any tree in the garden'?" (ESV)

The Lie

Scripture moves from Adam's joyous song in the previous chapter, 2:23, to Eve's alluring conversation with the serpent. After a vague and brief introduction, the serpent immediately moved in to spoil God's creation. In 2:16, God commanded Adam, prior to Eve's existence, that he may eat from every tree except from the tree of the knowledge of good and evil. This command was passed down to Eve either through Adam or through a conversation with God that was not recorded. Satan was testing Eve's knowledge and tempting her commitment. Satan was probing for a way in by using God's Word to his own advantage. In verse 3, Eve failed to mention the name of the tree she and Adam were forbidden to eat from. Obviously, Satan knew God's command not to eat from the tree of the knowledge of good and evil and chose to distort the truth. Once Eve let her guard down, Satan went in for the kill. Eve did not see what Satan was trying to accomplish and only focused on what she was forbidden to have.

P.O.I.

"Serpent"

Man and Woman were given the command to subdue and have dominion over all living things on the earth. This included the serpent!

Word Study

God: H430

'ĕlôhîym

el-o-heem'

Plural of 433; *gods* in the ordinary sense; but specifically used (in the plural thus, especially with the article) of the supreme *God*; occasionally applied by way of deference to *magistrates*; and sometimes as a superlative.

KJV Usage: angels, X exceeding, God (gods) (-dess, -ly), X (very) great, judges, X mighty. God above all "gods."

A plural form with a singular meaning.

Personal Application

It would be unwise to think that Satan or his demons do not know God's Word, and it would be equally unwise not to know God's Word yourself. Satan will disguise himself in ways you may not be prepared for, and, to be fair, it is impossible to know every trick Satan will use. But you do not need to worry about every trick he will use. Eve certainly did not realize what was about to take place, but it seemed clear she did not care about God's command or the desire to be obedient. She could only see at that moment what she wanted, and nothing else mattered. You have been given the Armor of God, so you must put it on! Although Adam and Eve were sin free, they were not free from temptation. Righteousness requires testing, so be ready at all times.

- How do you think Satan knew God's command?

- Why is it important to know God's Word when facing temptation?

- What are the differences between testing and temptation?

- Where is the Armor of God discussed in the Bible?

- Does the church need to do a better job teaching you about Satan and his demons?

- What were the consequences, if any, of the lie?

- Why do you think Satan didn't leave after Adam and Eve sinned? (Genesis 3:14 shows he stayed.)

- Are you committed to the truth regardless of any temptation?

Genesis 3:3

...but God said, 'You shall not eat of the fruit of the tree that is in the
midst of the garden, neither shall you touch it,
lest you die.'" (ESV)

P.O.I.

"Forbidden Fruit"

The pomegranate
is a strong
candidate.

Although the *fig
has its merits.

*see Genesis 3:7

The Lie

According to Genesis 2:17, before Eve was created, God commanded Adam that he should not eat from the tree of knowledge of good and evil. Notice that there is no mention of Eve's addendum, "touch it." There are three possibilities that determine whether Eve's statement was a lie or not. 1) Adam attached it to God's original command and

Eve's statement was made out of innocence (making Adam the liar). 2) Eve added it herself, making it an outright lie. 3) It was a command from God that the Scriptures do not record. (God's commands have always been clear, leaving the third possibility unlikely.)

Scripture does not say whether Eve received information about the Garden of Eden from God or

from Adam, but most would agree that Adam taught Eve what God had taught him. In any case, Eve broke the command, "you must not eat from it," and that was why she was held accountable.

Note that Scripture appears to affirm that Adam was present during the conversation between Eve and the "Serpent." His failure to stand on truth brought destruction.

Word Study
Die: H4191

[muwth /mooth/] v.
1a (Qal).

In dying you shall die

1a1 to die.

1a2 to die (as penalty), be put to death.

1a3 to die, perish (of a nation).

1a4 to die prematurely (by neglect of wise moral conduct).

1b (Polel) to kill, put to death, dispatch.

1c (Hiphil) to kill, put to death.

1d (Hophal).

1d1 to be killed, be put to death.

1d1a to die prematurely.

Personal Application

There is nothing wrong with self-regulations to help guide you to obedience. For example, Jesus said in Matthew 5:27-30 that "everyone who looks at a woman with lustful intent has already committed adultery with her in

his heart." It is clear that you cannot physically remove yourself from the world, but you can remove your mind from falling into its temptations. When you find yourself in a confrontation with lust, simply look

away, pray, and move to a different location. If going to a bar entices you to become intoxicated and look at other women, then do not go to bars. Life has its complications, so don't add to it if it is within your power.

- What are the problems with adding to God's commands?

- Are you trying to add to God's grace by adding to His commands? If so, how?

- Does adding to God's commands attempt to make you spiritually alive or does it deaden you?

- What are a couple's responsibilities to each other when it comes to obedience to God's commands?

- If your spouse, friend, or church member is sinning, what are your responsibilities?

- What were the consequences, if any, of the lie?

- How do we know the serpent was Satan?

Genesis 3:4-5

But the serpent said to the woman, "You will not surely die. For God knows that when you eat of it your eyes will be opened, and you will be like God, knowing good and evil." (ESV)

The Lie

It is not difficult to recognize the lies that Satan told. What's important to understand is the choice of lies. Satan certainly knows human weaknesses and is an expert at exploitation and word usage. Satan attacked Adam and Eve's human vulnerability, and he will certainly do the same to you. His attacks are aimed at getting you to fulfill your fleshly desires. Not only will Satan attack a person individually, he and his minions will attack entire church congregations. Satan's mission is simple: to steal, kill, and destroy. Each lie Satan tells will be unique to the individual and tailor-made in an attempt to prevent you from being a vessel for God. Like a thief, he will disguise himself so that he will be virtually unrecognizable to his victim. So, you must always be ready to stand resolute on the truth. Satan will also bring good things to your life, hoping that the little good he brought will prevent you from seeking out the best from God and for God.

Word Study

Good: H2896
[*towb* /tobe/]

Morally correct for its intended purpose;
Well-pleasing;
Proper

Personal Application

Satan is the best in the business when it comes to lies, but God's truth is supreme and absolute. The enemy knows exactly what to attempt to cast doubt upon you and your trust in God and His Word. But we have a way out from our human weakness, and that is our Savior and His Word!

Satan's lies are not random; he lies with a purpose. Just as you are to live life with the purpose of doing God's will, Satan has a purpose, too, in everything he does.

(See John 10:10)

We cannot stop temptation from seeking us out, but you can choose truth or you can choose sin. The Bible instructs every Christian to "stand firm" in their faith. The visual can be likened to a fighter's stance: one who is always ready for battle both physically and mentally, both offensive and defensive.

- Have you been able to recognize any recent attacks by the enemy?

- Why does standing against evil become difficult at times?

- How do you discern the difference between evil attacks vs. refinement by God?

- What lies did you tell recently, and what were the consequences?

- Are there personal consequences when standing on truth? Why?

- What were the consequences, if any, of the lie?

- Do you know your strengths and weaknesses? Why is it important to recognize them?

Genesis 4:9

Then the Lord said to Cain, "Where is your brother Abel?" "I don't know," he replied. "Am I my brother's guardian?" (HCSB)

P.O.I.

(John Scopes was arrested for teaching evolution during a school class.)

At the Scopes Trial in Tennessee in 1925, William Jennings Bryan, the prosecutor who stood for the Christian faith, failed to answer the question about who Cain's wife was, posed by the ACLU lawyer, Clarence Darrow.

*The answer to the question is that Cain's wife had to be his sister and not from another race that were separate from the descendant's of Adam and Eve.

The Lie

Cain and Abel were brothers, and during the course of time, each one brought an offering to God. Abel's offering pleased God, while Cain's offering did not. There has been speculation as to why Cain's offering did not please God, but Scripture points out that when each brought an offering, Cain's was noted as "an offering," while Abel's was noted as being the "firstborn."

It is clear that Cain did not give God the respect He deserved. Cain became so angry, that he killed his brother, and then he buried him. All too often, we are guided by feelings, rather than obedience and truth. In Cain's case, his feelings overwhelmed him, and, rather than seeking out forgiveness and repentance, he took matters into his own hands. You are not only your brother's guardian, but you have been given a great responsibility: to be the guardian of truth! If you are a Christian, then you have all the power you need to do what is right for the Lord.

(See 1 John 3:12 for further insight to this passage.)

Personal Application

As usual, a lie is followed by the excuse. Regardless of how we may feel that day, we are not released from our obligation to walk in the Spirit. We are not released from the excuses that we have, and we are certainly not released from being a guardian of all that God has blessed us with. Take note of the word study for "keeper." Notice that it does NOT say "when you feel like it." We are responsible because God graces us and commands us, and that should be good enough.

Feelings are a guide, but God is the Guiding Force.

God will always confront your sin, so why make excuses for it when He already knows?

Word Study
Keeper: H8104

[*shamar* /shaw·mar/]

to keep, guard, observe, give heed, to preserve and protect

- Free will can be both a blessing and a curse. Why?

- What has overwhelmed you recently that prevented you from doing the right thing?

- Think of some of the excuses you have come up with and then explain what the true consequences are.

- Are you mentoring someone?

- What are some of the steps you can take to become a true keeper of God's Word and his people?

- What were the consequences, if any, of the lie?

Genesis 4:24

If Cain is to be avenged seven times over, then for Lamech
it will be seventy-seven times! (HSCB)

P.O.I.

According to the Disaster Center, in 1960, there were 9,110 murders in the United States. In 2011, there were 14,612.

The Lie

In 4:8, Cain killed his brother Abel. Because of God's grace, He spares Cain from any immediate human repercussion by placing a mark on him. Lamech is a descendant from the line of Cain, and he also commits a murder after apparently being assaulted by another man. Scripture does not indicate this was self-defense, but rather a vengeful act on the part of Lamech. His twisted logic forces him to believe that God will avenge and protect him even more so than God did for Cain. He believed his own lie that not only would his sin go unpunished, but God would avenge anyone who would harm him. Lamech justifies his crime and goes even further by bragging about it to his wives. In this verse, we can see that Lamech's personal interpretation of God's love and grace causes him to rejoice in his sin.

Word Study
Murder: G5408 (*phonos*)

murder, slaughter, killing.
(intentional, unjustified homicide)

Personal Application

Just because you believe something to be true does not make it the truth. The concept "*truth for you*" distorts the absoluteness of God. Truth cannot be altered just because we don't agree with it. How God deals with one person cannot always be applied to the next person. The Scriptures were given to us for our guide to holiness, our guide to fellowship, and our guide to salvation. When we misapply God's Word to fit our sinful ways, the truth no longer remains in us. (See 1 John 1:6–10) When we brag about being under God's protection, we tend to cloak our sinful behavior in the name of grace. Lack of punishment from God does not mean He approves of our behavior. It simply means we have distorted the truth and are living under His patience.

- If truth could be altered, what assurances do we really have?

- What were the consequences, if any, of the lie?

- Study 1 John 1:6-10.

- If a person does not agree with God's Word, how should that be handled?

- If a Christian brags about sin, how would you deal with that situation? (See Matthew 18:15-20)

- Would you consider Lamech's statement a lie?

- Is misinterpreting God necessarily a lie?

- Do you get upset when you see God "ignoring" the sins of others?

Genesis 12:12-13

When the Egyptians see you, they will say, 'This is his wife.' They will kill me but let you live. 'Please say you're my sister so it will go well for me because of you, and my life will be spared on your account." (HCSB)

P.O.I.
We typically visualize a harem as a group of wives belonging to one man, but the term "harem" can be used to describe an area as well—a religious harem. Mecca was once a religious harem, where only Muslims were allowed.

The Lie

Planning and execution! Scripture introduces us to Abram (Abraham) through the genealogy in chapter 11. Then in chapter 12, we are introduced to Abram as being called by God. In the first few verses of chapter 12, God tells Abram that he will be blessed and made into a great nation. By verse 12, Abram disregarded what God just said and started freaking out because of the Egyptians; more specifically, because of Sarai's (Sarah) beauty. As Abram ventured into Egypt, he told his wife to tell everyone that she was his sister. That was the planning stage. Eventually, Pharaoh took Sarai into his harem, and this caused the Lord to strike Pharaoh and his house with plagues. The execution part of this plan occurred between verses 13 and 19. Though Scripture doesn't specify how, the pharaoh discovered Abram's deceit; only then did Abram confess his sin. The consequence of his actions led the pharaoh's men to escort Abram, Sarai, and everything that belonged to them out of Egypt in disgrace.

Word Study
Well: H3190

[*yatab* /yaw·**tab**/]

to make glad, rejoice, to do good to, deal well with, to do well, do thoroughly, to make a thing good or right or beautiful, to do well, do right.

In the context of this scripture, the words used with "well" describe an act of self-preservation.

Personal Application

It seems that self-preservation is the most common reason for lying. In Abraham's case, he was looking out for his own best interest and certainly not the interest of his wife. Notice that even after Pharaoh took Sarah, Abraham didn't come forth with the truth and get his wife! You must think through every decision you make to see if it is wise or unwise, whether self-preserving or for the glory of God. Being obedient to the truth can come at a personal cost, but you can rest in the joy of the Spirit if that cost was truth-preserving. Sin affects more than just you!

Luke 7:35 says, "Yet wisdom is vindicated by all her children." (HCSB) What do you think that means?

- When is the best time to confess a sin you have committed?

- If confession comes only after the sin is discovered, are you truly repentant of the sin or the discovery?

- What were the consequences, if any, of the lie?

- Every true Christian knows his or her own destination, so why is the journey such a struggle?

- Imagine your life if you had never spoken a particular lie that caused a great consequence. Was it worth it?

- When you fail to believe God, does that make it a lie? (Abram thought he would be killed.)

Genesis 16:5

Then Sarai said to Abram, "You are responsible for my suffering! I put my slave in your arms, and ever since she saw that she was pregnant, she has treated me with contempt. May the Lord judge between me and you." (HCSB)

The Lie

The best way to describe this event is to take it directly from the Scriptures. Genesis 16:1–5 (ESV), "Now Sarai, Abram's wife, had borne him no children. She had a female Egyptian servant whose name was Hagar. And Sarai said to Abram, "Behold now, the Lord has prevented me from bearing children. Go in to my servant;

it may be that I shall obtain children by her." And Abram listened to the voice of Sarai. So, after Abram had lived ten years in the land of Canaan, Sarai, Abram's wife, took Hagar the Egyptian, her servant, and gave her to Abram her husband as a wife. And he went in to Hagar, and she conceived. And when she saw that she had conceived,

she looked with contempt on her mistress. And Sarai said to Abram, "May the wrong done to me be on you! I gave my servant to your embrace, and when she saw that she had conceived, she looked on me with contempt. May the Lord judge between you and me!" (HCSB says, "You are responsible for my suffering.")

Word Study
Suffering: H2555 violence, wrong

wrong, including injurious language, harsh treatment, etc.

Personal Application

Today, we call this type of behavior from Sarai "blame shifting." We have to call this for what it is, and that is a lie. We cannot excuse our behavior by attempting to blame someone else. We then minimize our responsibility and try to place it on someone else.

Sarai brought this upon herself, and although Hagar—and even Abram—didn't help the situation, Sarai initiated all this by bringing Abram and Hagar together. When we want something, we can have the tendency to do whatever it takes to get what we want regardless of

future consequences. By human nature, we can understand this logic. But God makes it clear that we are accountable for our own actions regardless of the actions of someone else. We are no longer under the power of sin; we are under the power of the Holy Spirit.

- What were the consequences, if any, of the lie?

- Why do we blame others for things we did ourselves?

- Is blame shifting a lie?

- Why did Abram listen to Sarai?

- Why do you think Abram didn't stop the bickering between Hagar and Sarai?

- Did Sarai "covet" a child?

- When something doesn't go your way, how do you respond?

- How does God want you to respond?

Genesis 18:15

Sarah was afraid, so she lied and said, "I did not laugh."
But he said, "Yes, you did laugh." (NIV)

The Lie

The Lord appeared to Abraham and told him that He would return "at this time next year; and behold, Sarah your wife will have a son." (NASB) Upon hearing the news that she is going to bear a child, she laughs at this prophetic miracle. It is unknown if the laugh was audible or not. The wording of Scripture makes it seem likely that the laugh was "within" herself and therefore inaudible to anyone else. But, as we all know, God hears all things aloud and within the hearts and minds of people. When God asked Abraham (suggesting an audible laugh) why Sarah laughed, Sarah quickly denied it. Scripture gives the reason for this lie: fear. Like Abraham, Sarah kicked into self-preservation mode and decided to lie her way out, rather than being honest with God. What makes this verse so exciting is that God immediately confronted Sarah with her lie and then went on to complete His mission—judge Sodom and Gomorrah. In other words, confronting Sarah was just as important to God as judging an entire nation.

Personal Application

Can't you just imagine Sarah behind the tent door holding a glass up to her ear while intently trying to listen to what was being said? When Sarah's prayers were answered, she did not run out and praise God and do a dance. Nope, she laughed; doubting God's Word and underestimating His power while overestimating her humanity. Do we really believe that if we lie, God will somehow not catch it? Do we really believe that we can better protect ourselves more than the Creator can? Truth should not be feared because God truly desires a repentant and broken vessel. God does not have bigger and better things to deal with; YOU are His bigger and better.

Word Study
Afraid: H3372
[yare' /yaw ray/]

to fear, revere, dread, be afraid

filled with fear or apprehension

filled with concern or regret over an unwanted situation

- Why do you think God took the time to confront Sarah when His primary mission at that point was Sodom, Gomorrah, and the surrounding cities?

- Does God confronting your sin create in you a repentant heart or a hardened one? Why?

- Why do you think fear is such a powerful force?

- What were the consequences, if any, of the lie?

- Joseph, Mary's husband, is one example of not letting fear guide decisions. Why? (Matthew 1:19-20)

_____
_____
_____
_____
_____
_____
_____
_____
_____
_____
_____
_____
_____
_____
_____
_____
_____
_____
_____
_____
_____
_____
_____
_____
_____
_____
_____
_____

Genesis 20:2

And Abraham said of Sarah his wife, "She is my sister." And Abimelech king of Gerar sent and took Sarah. (ESV)

P.O.I.

We are lied to about 200 times each day. Most people lie to others once or twice a day and deceive about 30 people per week.
The average is 7 times per hour if you count all the times people lie to themselves.
We lie in 30 to 38 percent of all our interactions.
College students lie in 50 percent of conversations with their mothers.

The Lie

Once again, the lie is obvious. Approximately twenty-five years after Abraham left Egypt, he and his family settled in Gerar and were met by Abimelech, the king of that land. As you remember in chapter 12, Abraham told this same lie to Pharaoh, but Scripture did not say how the pharaoh discovered the truth. In this case, Scripture reveals that God came to Abimelech in a dream and exposed Abraham's deceit. After being warned by God to restore Sarah, Abraham was confronted by Abimelech. In disgrace, Abraham was rebuked by the pagan king. Abraham's reason for the lie was noted in verses 11–13. (See Genesis 20:11) The most interesting portion of this chapter is that God "closed all the wombs of the household of Abimelech" and told him that he would be a "dead man because of the woman (Sarah)."

A pagan king innocent and a Christian prophet guilty, yet Abimelech is the one being punished because of the lie. Even though God protected Sarah and kept Abimelech from sinning, Abraham, nonetheless, had to pray for Abimelech's restoration.

Word Study

Wife: H802
['ishshah /ish·shaw/]

The Hebrew language's most common word for "wife" or "woman."

The origin of woman is explained in Genesis 2:23, 24. She is depicted as the physical counterpart of man deserving of his unswerving loyalty.

Personal Application

It is thought-provoking and even mind-boggling to consider that a lie AFFECTS and EFFECTS the INNOCENT! When you are faced with the option of telling the truth or telling a lie, think about not only how much damage it could cause, especially on your relationship with Christ, but the likely consequences of your action. Do you really want to cause other's pain by protecting your own self-interest? The thought of Abraham allowing his wife to be taken is incomprehensible!

In Abraham's pursuit of self-protection, he not only subjected himself to possible consequences, but he also put Sarah in a position of temptation by allowing Abimelech to take her as a wife. This action would have undoubtedly led Sarah to adultery.

- What were the consequences, if any, of the lie?

- Is there such a thing as a justifiable lie in God's eyes? For example: A man breaks into your home and asks if you are alone, and you say "yes," knowing your family is in the other room. A police officer lies to a child's rapist to illicit a confession?

- State and federal laws allow police officers to lie to a suspect within reason. If the law allows it, does God consider it a sin?

Suggested
Reading:
Gen 25:19-34

Genesis 25:32

P.O.I.
Lentil Soup

Lentil is a small,
pealike plant. Its
pods turn
reddish-brown
when boiled.

Esau said, "I am about to die; of what use is a birthright to me?" (ESV)

The Lie

While Jacob was cooking some stew, Esau came in from the field and begged for some of the food Jacob was preparing. Without hesitation, Jacob demanded Esau's birthright in exchange for some stew. Unwilling to think things through, Esau claimed he was about to die, sold Jacob his birthright, and ate. (You have to wonder how long Jacob had been "cooking" up this plan!)

It is highly unlikely Esau was going to die at that moment if he did not eat something. The Scripture goes on to say that "Esau despised his birthright." Esau did not see the privilege he had as firstborn, nor did he recognize that God had a plan for him. He carelessly disregarded his position, lied to get his way in the heat of the moment, and was subsequently described as unholy in Hebrews 12:16. Although Jacob's actions are questionable, God's punishment rested on Esau. The blatant disregard for, and the selling of, Esau's birthright fulfilled God's decree that the older (Esau) shall serve the younger (Jacob); thus, Israel's twelve tribes were born from Jacob and not from Esau.

Word Study
Birthright: H1062

bᵉkôrâh bᵉkôrâh

bek-o-raw', bek-o-raw'

Feminine of 1060; the *firstling* of man or beast; abstractly *primogeniture*: birthright, firstborn (-ling).

Personal Application

How many times have you said, "God, if you help me through this, I promise…." During the heat of the moment is precisely when our faith should be at its best. It is easy to have faith in God when you have something to eat, can pay your bills, your children are healthy, and you have a job (See Mark 9:24). God's plans for our lives do not change with OUR circumstances, but it seems our faith does. No matter what situation you find yourself in today, praise God in your times of trouble. Think about this: when everything is said and done, you GET to spend eternity with Jesus! Therefore, you must guard your words carefully and apply your faith in every situation.

- Why wasn't Jacob punished for his trickery?

- Was there a consequence(s) for Jacob's actions?

- Promises made in tears to God are difficult to keep. Why?

- Are you willing to trust God in your darkest hour?

- What were the consequences, if any, of the lie?

- Is exaggeration still a lie?

- Who determines what a lie is?

- At one time, people believed the world was flat and even taught it. Is a worldwide belief still a lie?

Genesis 26:7

When the men of that place asked him about his wife, he said, "She is my sister," because he was afraid to say, "She is my wife." He thought, "The men of this place might kill me on account of Rebekah, because she is beautiful." (NIV)

The Lie

Although Isaac had not been born at the time of Abraham's similar sin, Isaac committed the same act as his father. The Lord just told Isaac that He would "confirm the oath I swore to your father Abraham." Isaac had nothing to fear, yet fear replaced the promises of God.

Apparently, the lie went on for quite some time (see verse 8), but Isaac and Rebekah became careless and were caught. Certainly, telling a lie is much easier than living it out to keep the truth from surfacing. The pagan king confronted God's chosen in verse 9, and

Isaac confessed the reason for the lie. Abimelech decreed that no man shall touch Rebekah or they shall be put to the death. With all of that, Isaac wasn't forced out of the kingdom in disgrace; rather, he stayed in the land with the hand of God blessing him in all things.

P.O.I.
The Abimelech Isaac was confronted by was not the same Abimelech who confronted Abraham. He was probably a son or grandson.

Word Study
Pagan: G1484 [ethnos /eth·nos/]

In the OT, foreign nations not worshipping the true God.

One who has little or no religion and who delights in sensual pleasures and material goods; an irreligious or hedonistic person.

Personal Application

The one thing you never have to teach a child to do is sin! Even though Isaac is blessed by God, notice that Scripture records that all the blessings come only after the lie is confronted and confessed. It is so easy to place your

circumstances in two categories: testing by God or temptation by Satan. Life isn't as simple as A and B as we wish it were sometimes. If the circumstances in your life are less than desirable, then do not neglect the fact that *you* may have caused

them by your own volition. If the blessings of God seem unimaginable, then look deeply within yourself. Confront and confess all the sins you have been hiding. God will honor your obedience.

- Have you recognized any sinful patterns or traits within your own family?

- If so, what can you do to stop the cycle of this repeating pattern of sins?

- Knowledge of your sins is only part of the solution. Can you explain what the rest of the solutions are?

- Should you tell your children, family, or friends about your sinful past? Why or why not (positive and negative)?

- God gives you a testimony. What is its purpose?

- What were the consequences, if any, of the lie?

Genesis 27:19

Jacob said to his father, "I am Esau your firstborn;
I have done as you told me now sit up and eat of my game,
that your soul may bless me." (ESV)

The Lie

Chapter 27 is full of deceit! Isaac believed he was going to die very soon, so he called out to his older son, his firstborn, Esau, to prepare a meal. After the meal was eaten, Isaac would then give Esau his blessing. Rebekah overheard this conversation and told Jacob, in essence, to deceive his father and switch places with Esau. Rebekah wanted Jacob to receive the blessing entitled to the firstborn. Rebekah put skins of young goats on Jacob to simulate Esau's hairy body. The ruse worked and Jacob, through deception, received the blessing. Once the lie was discovered by Isaac and Esau, Jacob had to flee for his life from his brother, and, for that, he was never able to see his mother again. As you will see in 27:32, Esau still didn't take any responsibility for his actions. Back in Chapter 25, the Lord had already made the pronouncement that the younger would serve the older, and so the Lord was going to continue His oath that He started with Abraham through Jacob. It wasn't until the death of Isaac that the two brothers came together. And even then, Esau showed great forgiveness, while Jacob still exhibited distrust.

Personal Application

Jacob was initially reserved about doing as his mother told him, but Rebekah assured him that she would take on any curse that would befall Jacob. Even though there was no "curse," Jacob was on the run from that day forward.

This whole chapter begs the question that is posed on the next page: should you obey the voice of a liar even when the liar is your parent? Well, we would say that the obvious answer is "no," but respect for a family member at that time was much, much different than the respect we give our families today. Respect was taken much more seriously, and obedience to a parent was nonnegotiable.

P.O.I.
Being recognized as the firstborn granted a person special entitlements such as double the inheritance of the family assets. Study out "firstborn" to really understand your position in Christ.

Word Study

Firstborn: H1060

[bâkowr /bek·ore/]
First brought
forth; eldest

In the context of this scripture, it simply means the "oldest."

G4416

[prototokos
/pro·tot·ok·os]
This Greek word for "firstborn" is used as a title or rank: king, first over all creation—Jesus is the firstborn.

- Should you obey the voice of a liar (see Genesis 27:13)?

- Scripture clearly says you are to honor and obey your parents, but is there a situation where you must be disobedient?

- If you are having family problems because of a lie, or even a misunderstanding, is there anything you can do about it to make amends?

- Why is it that most people feel more comfortable telling a lie over telling the truth?

- Why do you get angry when someone lies to you even though you may have lied?

- What were the consequences, if any, of the lie?

Suggested Reading:

Gen. 29:1-30

Genesis 29:23

But in the evening he took his daughter Leah and brought her to Jacob, and he went in to her. (ESV)

P.O.I.

Twelve Tribes of Israel (Jacob):

Asher
Benjamin
Dan
Gad
Issachar
Joseph
Judah
Levi
Naphtali
Reuben
Simeon
Zebulun

The Lie

It is not difficult to see the lie, but it is difficult to pinpoint the necessary verse for this study (see Genesis 29:19). This lie was a lie by action, but necessary to be discussed. Rebekah told Jacob to flee to her brother, Laban. When Jacob arrived in the land, he met Rachel and fell in love. Laban agreed to give Rachel to Jacob if only he would serve Laban for seven years.

Jacob agreed to the marriage arrangements and worked the agreed seven years. After the terms ended, Jacob asked for Rachel as promised, but Laban snuck Rachel's older sister, Leah, into the bedroom of Jacob instead. Jacob didn't realize he had been defrauded until the morning. Jacob confronted Laban's deceit, and Laban reasoned it was not

the practice of that place to give the youngest before the oldest. Laban told Jacob he was to complete a week with Leah, and then after a week, he would give him Rachel. But even then, he was to work another seven years once he received Rachel as his wife. Jacob agreed and after fourteen years, he was released of any contractual agreement with Laban.

Word Study

Lie: H8266

[shaqar /shaw·kar/]

H8267

[sheqer /sheh·ker/]

to deal falsely

lie, deception, disappointment, falsehood; deception (what deceives or disappoints or betrays one); deceit, fraud, wrong; fraudulently, wrongfully (as adverb); falsehood (injurious in testimony); testify falsehood, false oath, swear falsely; falsity (of false or self-deceived prophets); lie, falsehood (in general); false tongue; in vain.

Personal Application

"What comes around goes around." "The deceiver becomes the deceived." "You got what you deserved." "You reap what you sow."

If this isn't a lesson on why NOT to tell a lie, then what is? A lesson needed to be taught, and Jacob

was the student. There is no doubt that Jacob remembered all the times he was the author of his deceptive ways. When we are lied to by someone, we feel violated. We feel belittled and we feel angered.

So remember those feelings the next time you consider telling a lie, and let those feelings be a guide and reason why you should NEVER lie to anyone! You may be the recipient of the lies, but don't become the author of them.

- Are you obligated to fulfill your promise even under fraudulent arrangements? In other words, are you obligated to keep your promise even though you were lied to?

- Is making a promise wrong?

- Why do people use "to tell you the truth" in sentences?

- Do people trust what you tell them? In other words, does your yes mean yes?

- If people don't trust your word, can you effectively evangelize?

- What were the consequences, if any, of the lie?

- Genesis 29:26 appears to be the justification of the lie. What do you think?

Genesis 30:35

But that day Laban removed the male goats that were striped and spotted, and all the female goats that were speckled and spotted, everyone that had white on it, and every lamb that was black, and put them in the charge of his sons. (ESV)

P.O.I.
Speckled and spotted sheep, lambs, and goats were considered inferior animals.

The Lie

Jacob was ready to start his own household and wanted to leave with Leah and Rachel. But Laban realized that the Lord was blessing Jacob in everything he did; therefore, Laban was prospering off Jacob. Because of Laban's deceitful and greedy nature, he was unwilling to give up Jacob! Jacob's wages would be all the striped, speckled, spotted, and black goats, lambs, and sheep. Jacob traveled three days distance between him and Laban and began to pasture his own flock as well as Laban's. In verse 35 (above), you will see what happened next. Although this is not an outright lie, it is nonetheless a lie by action. Laban continued to treat Jacob unfairly, and, once again, changed the terms of agreement.

Word Study

Work: H5647

'âbad

aw-bad'

A primitive root; to *work* (in any sense); by implication to *serve, till,* (causatively) *enslave,* etc.: - X be, keep in bondage, be bondmen, bond-service, compel, do, dress, ear, execute, + husbandman, keep, labour (-ing man), bring to pass, (cause to, make to) serve (-ing, self), (be, become) servant (-s), do (use) service, till (-er), transgress [from margin], (set a) work, be wrought, worshipper.

Personal Application

How many times has your boss changed something without your approval? Could you continue to work for such a person as Jacob did for Laban? Jacob had a goal, the right frame of mind, and the faith and trust in the Lord to get him through. Changes will occur and not every one will be in your favor. Yet it is your responsibility to continue to work for the Lord as though nothing else matters. God will take care of you as he did for Jacob. God's blessings are not just reserved for the faithful who were recorded in the Bible. God will continue to bless the faithful even today.

- Is a lie by action still a lie?

- If I say I will help you move your furniture but fail to show up, is that a lie or something else?

- Do you have a story like Jacob? How did you get through it?

- See Genesis 33:12-17 for another example of a lie by action. Do you think Jacob's actions were justified?

- What were the consequences, if any, of the lie?

Suggested Reading:
Gen. 31:1-55

Genesis 31:35

Rachel said to her father, "Don't be angry, my lord, that I cannot stand up in your presence; I'm having my period." So he searched but could not find the household gods. (NIV)

P.O.I.
The distance between Padan-aram and Mount Gilead was a little over 300 miles. Jacob must have traveled between 40–45 miles a day.

The Lie

Jacob took his family and his possessions and fled from Laban. Just before, when Laban went away to shear the sheep, Rachel stole her father's household gods. After Laban pursued Jacob and caught up with him, he accused Jacob of the theft. Not knowing what Rachel did, Jacob defended himself and even made a bold declaration that if Laban ever finds his gods, he would have that person put to death. Laban searched the area and got to Rachel. Rachel had placed the gods inside her camel's saddle. She refused to come down off the animal and made up the lie to protect herself. Laban did not find the gods, and Jacob, after years of being used, laid into Laban with all his frustration.

It is unknown why Rachel took the household gods, but three reasons seem logical: it was the only inheritance she believed she would receive from her father's estate; she believed it would protect her and her family on the journey; or she was not ready to give up her own idolatry.

Word Study
Angry: H2734

charah
(khaw-raw')

to burn or be kindled with anger

Personal Application

Rachel did not get caught, nor did she confess her sin afterwards. It is difficult to tell whether Rachel feared her father's wrath, feared giving up what she had stolen, or feared Jacob's threat of putting the person responsible to death.

Whatever reason Rachel had, she feared the potential outcome of her actions over the fear of God. God doesn't promise He will get you out of every circumstance you put yourself into, but He certainly values the truth over our own protection.

In some sense, it is like a child who gets caught doing something and then tells the truth. Are they truly sorry for their actions, or are they just sorry they got caught? Confession of sin, prior to getting caught, is always the godly way.

- What were the consequences, if any, of the lie?

- Do you have any household gods in your home?

- What is an idol?

- Can anything become an idol?

- What does God value more, confession of sin prior to getting caught or after getting caught?

- Have you ever lied to cover up your sins?

- Are there still sins from your past that you have not confessed to?

- Should a person seek amends from someone they sinned against even if it has been years since the sin?

Genesis 33:14

Let my lord pass on ahead of his servant, and I will lead on slowly, at the pace of the livestock that are ahead of me and at the pace of the children, until I come to my lord in Seir. (ESV)

P.O.I.
In other cultures, referring to a male as "lord" was a sign of respect and submission. The use of "sir" today still carries respect but not necessarily submission.

The Lie

After reconciling with Esau, Jacob told his brother to go ahead of him and that he would meet up with him at Seir. Jacob had no intention of going that direction but instead moved on to Succoth. Even after approximately twenty-one years of separation, the trust had not been repaired. Certainly, Jacob could have claimed God was calling him in another direction. The meeting was divine intervention, and rather than making the best of it, Jacob continued to concentrate on his own self-preservation. God has reconciled us to Himself through Jesus Christ, but change comes in time. Time itself does not cause the change, but the Holy Spirit guides us through our trials and tribulations. A concentrated effort must take place for maturity to take shape.

Word Study
Restoration: H7725

shub (shoob)

to turn back return

Personal Application

Reconciliation does not guarantee restoration of trust. As a matter of fact, it takes hard work to restore trust in another person, even a blood relative. It is not uncommon to get "burnt" by someone and then have the mind-set that all people are the same. Once trust has been broken by an individual, it can be difficult to trust anyone. People will fail us all the time, and although that should not be an excuse for others to let us down, our hope and trust should be in Christ Jesus! When a person fails you, try not to blame Jesus. Human nature if flawed, but the nature of Christ is truth. Rest assured, God will not lead you astray when others do.

- Can you truly forgive someone and still not trust them?

- When people fail you, do you also lose trust in Christ?

- R and R: reconciliation and restoration. Explain the difference?

- What were the consequences, if any, of the lie?

- Should you trust someone first, or should they earn your trust? In other words, should trust be granted immediately or upon proven experience?

Genesis 34:15

Only on this condition will we agree with you—that you will become as we are by every male among you being circumcised. (ESV)

The Lie

Verse 13 proves verses 15–16 was the lie, and it was carried out in verse 25. Shechem saw Dinah and became infatuated or deeply attracted to her. The Scriptures record that Shechem took Dinah and raped her! When Dinah's brothers heard of what happened to their sister, they became angry and plotted revenge. Hamor, the father of Shechem, tried to negotiate with the brothers to allow Dinah to marry Shechem. Jacob's sons lied to Hamor and told him that they would give Dinah away in marriage only if he and every male in the land would become circumcised. Jacob's sons reasoned that if they were to do this, they would become like them, and, by that act, God's law would allow the intermarriage.

This seemed to please Hamor and Shechem, and when all the males had become circumcised and were hurting after the "surgery," Jacob's sons, Simeon and Levi, went into the gates of the city when the men were at their weakest point and slaughtered every male by sword.

Word Study
Defiled: H2930

[tame' /taw·may'/]

to be or become unclean-sexually, religiously, ceremonially

to corrupt the purity or perfection of

This same Hebrew word used to describe what happened to Dinah is the same word used to describe profaning the name of God!

Personal Application

People claim there is no absolute truth, even though this statement, in and of itself, would be considered absolute by its own definition. Well, here is an absolutely true statement that NO ONE should debate; THERE IS ABSOLUTELY NO JUSTIFICATION FOR RAPING ANYONE! It is disturbing when people pervert justice in the name of God. For instance, you may have an opinion about whether abortion should be legal or not, but by no means should anyone have the right to "blow up" an abortion clinic in the name of God. No wonder people distrust Christians when people use God's Word for their own agenda. Romans 12:19 says, "Beloved, never avenge yourselves, but leave it to the wrath of God, for it is written, 'Vengeance is mine, I will repay, says the Lord.'" (See Deut. 32:35.)

- Why do you think revenge can seemingly be a more powerful force than obedience to God?

- What was the cost of Simeon and Levi's sin? (See Genesis 49:5-7.)

- Why do you think it is important to forgive your offender if you were raped? (One reason is that lack of forgiveness allows the offender to continue the violation in the mind of the victim.)

- Was Jacob too harsh on Simeon and Levi?

- What were the consequences, if any, of the lie?

Genesis 37:20

"Come now, let's kill him and throw him into one of these cisterns and say that a ferocious animal devoured him. Then we'll see what comes of his dreams." (NIV)

P.O.I.
A varicolored tunic or tunic of many colors was a special robe worn by the person whom the father intended to be the future leader of the household.

The Lie

This lie had been proven out in verse 32. Joseph enjoyed being Israel's (Jacob) favorite son, but, in this process, Joseph became a bit arrogant. Joseph had a couple of dreams in which his parents and his brothers were submissive to him. The dreams showed his family bowing to Joseph, and, when he told them the dreams that he had, his brother's became angry and plotted his demise. Initially,

they were going to kill Joseph and tell their father that Joseph's death was the act of a wild beast. When Reuben heard this, he convinced his brother's not to kill him but throw him into a pit. Reuben's intent was to rescue Joseph from the pit later on, but, as it turned out, his brothers, after throwing him into the pit, retrieved him themselves and sold Joseph into slavery.

Joseph had to have known that his brothers did not like him, so to add insult to injury was just plain stupid on his part. Joseph's brothers were jealous of him and eventually hated him. Having just one of those feelings is detrimental in a person's life, but having both of those negative feelings is simply a dangerous combination.

Word Study

Varicolored Tunic:
H6446
[pac /pas/]

H3801 כְּתֹנֶת
[kâthoneth, kuttoneth
/keth·o·neth/]

a robe, undergarment or long shirt typically reaching from the palms of the hands to the soles of one feet.

Personal Application

Here is a good example of someone planning to sin, but, at this point, not having yet carried it out. Although the lie of intent was eventually made good, we should also focus on the thought process. In this verse, Joseph's brothers

were simply talking among themselves out of anger. The problem with this kind of talk is that it sets your mind not on the things of Christ, but on worldly things. As James 1:14 states, "Then when lust has conceived, it gives birth to sin; and

when sin is accomplished, it brings forth death." (NASB) This is precisely why when you are in the "heat of the moment," you must submit to the Holy Spirit and not the flesh. It is extremely difficult but not impossible.

- Is it a sin if you plan to do something illegal or immoral but do not carry it out?

- Is it a sin to lie to yourself? If so, give some examples.

- Like Joseph, Paul was thrown into prison for "no reason." Could you be an effective witness for God if you were wrongfully accused of a crime and thrown into prison?

- Have you ever been wrongfully accused of something?

- Have you ever planned to sin but not carried it any further?

- What were the consequences, if any, of the lie?

Suggested Reading:
Gen. 37:1-36

Genesis 37:31-32

So they took Joseph's tunic, and slaughtered a male goat and dipped the tunic in the blood; and they sent the varicolored tunic and brought it to their father and said, "We found this; please examine it to see whether it is your son's tunic or not." (NASB)

The Lie

This is the continuation of the previous study of Genesis 37:20. Here, the conception of the lie gave birth. When Reuben discovered that Joseph was not in the pit and had been sold into slavery, he and his brothers made good on their idea to tell their father that Joseph had been killed by a wild beast. As the verse above describes, they killed a goat and passed it off as Joseph's blood. They brought the tunic to Israel (Jacob) and told their father that they had found it. Israel did not ask any further questions about what may have happened, but assumed that Joseph had been killed by the beast based on the evidence he had at the time. Even though Joseph's brothers were prepared to tell their father the lie, they did not have to. The ruse worked so well that the assumption of Joseph's death had been committed into Israel's mind. The sin was so depraved that Joseph's brothers would rather see their father in depression and pain than tell the truth. Is living with someone else's pain easier than confession?

P.O.I.

Stress can cause sleep disorder, anxiety, loss of concentration, unhealthy weight gain or weight loss, weaken the immune system, and can be a key to heart disease and high blood pressure. (This is a partial list.)

Word Study

Worry: H3309

[merimnao /mer·im·nah·o]

to be anxious; to be troubled with cares; to care for; look out for (a thing); to seek to promote one's interests.

To struggle, fret, strangle, or choke.

The word carries a meaning that you are literally killing yourself over the worry or stress you are not releasing to God.

Personal Application

Can you imagine watching your parents suffer, or even your children suffer, and do nothing about it if you had the ability? Do not be afraid to stand up and admit fault, especially if it can save another from short or long-term pain.

Another important factor we can glean from this is favoritism. You can see the implications in this verse. Remember, the consequences of favoritism typically do not happen immediately. The teen years are a critical point in a person's life: physically, spiritually, and emotionally. Human suffering is certainly within God's sovereign plan, and, in many cases, we can do nothing about it. What we can do is stand fast in truth and try to make right any wrong.

- Have you truly put your suffering into perspective?

- Does suffering lead to repentance?

- Is there anyone you know whom you could help comfort?

- Do you, when you are hurting, cry out to God or become hard-hearted?

- Before you sin, is there such thing as a "point of no return"? For example: Joseph's brothers could have ended the lie at anytime.

- What were the consequences, if any, of the lie?

Suggested
Reading:
Gen. 38:1-30

Genesis 38:14

So she removed her widow's garments and covered herself with a veil, and wrapped herself, and sat in the gateway of Enaim, which is on the road to Timnah; for she saw that Shelah had grown up, and she had not been given to him as a wife. (NASB)

P.O.I.
Some customs required the wearing of widow garments (black) for an entire year and one day. A widow could not even leave the house except to attend church.

The Lie

Tamar, who was Judah's daughter-in-law, had a husband named Er. Er acted evil in the sight of the Lord, so He took his life. When Er died, it was the responsibility of Onan, Er's brother, to take Tamar as his wife and give her a child. But because of custom, Onan's offspring would be treated as though they were his older brother's instead. This did not please Onan, so he wasted his seed on the ground rather than giving Tamar a child. This angered the Lord, and He took his life as well. Judah then promised Tamar that if she would wait, he would give to her Shelah, another of his sons, when he got older. Tamar agreed, but when the time came for Shelah to be with her, Judah did not follow through with his promise. Tamar took matters into her own hands. She passed herself off as a prostitute and waited for Judah. When Judah went looking for a prostitute, he came to Tamar. Judah did not know it was her. During this sexual encounter, Tamar became pregnant. Eventually, it was discovered she was playing the harlot and was ordered to be put to death.

Word Study
Integrity: H8549

tamiym/taw·meem
complete, whole, entire, sound; complete, whole, entire; whole, sound, healthful; complete, entire (of time); sound, wholesome, unimpaired, innocent, having integrity; what is complete or entirely in accord with truth and fact.
Doing what is right when no one else is looking.

Personal Application

If you read on, you will discover that Tamar was not put to death. She told Judah she was the prostitute he had slept with and even had his ring, cord, and staff as proof. Although Tamar's actions are not justified, you can see what happens when you do not follow through with your promises to someone. If you are not a man or woman of your word, you do have the power within you to change it. Change is slow and trust is earned, so take every opportunity to slowly but intentionally become a respected person of trust and godliness. There are many ways to represent Christ to others, and showing integrity is just one of them.

- In your own words, define "integrity."

- What is the difference between integrity and ethics?

- Read Ruth 4:18-22 and Matthew 1:3 and explain what blessings came out of this sin?

- God is still God regardless of our hypocrisy and sin. How would you explain that to someone who was not a Christian?

- What were the consequences, if any, of the lie?

Suggested Reading:
Gen. 39:1-23

Genesis 39:14-15

...she called her household servants. "Look," she said to them, "this Hebrew has been brought to us to make sport of us! He came in here to sleep with me, but I screamed. When he heard me scream for help, he left his cloak beside me and ran out of the house." (NIV)

The Lie

When Joseph was sold into slavery, he came to be a slave to an Egyptian named Potiphar. Joseph was so blessed by God that he became the overseer of Potiphar's house and all that he owned. Over the course of time, his master's wife desired Joseph and tried to entice him to have sexual relations with her. Joseph refused! Then one day, Joseph went into his master's house to do some work when he was met once again by his master's wife. She grabbed him by his garments and demanded that Joseph sleep with her. Joseph took off running, but his garment was left behind in the hand of this woman. The trap was laid against Joseph, and the woman called the men of her husband's household and told them the lie. She said Joseph came into the house to have sexual relations with her. But when he tried, she screamed, and Joseph took off running. Afterward, her husband came home, and she told him her lies. The husband was so angry, he had Joseph thrown into prison. But once again, God was with Joseph, and the chief jailer put Joseph in charge of all who were in the jail.

Word Study
Fled: H5127 [nuwc /noos/]

to flee; to escape; to take flight; depart; disappear; to fly (to the attack) on horseback; to drive at; to take flight; to put to flight; to drive hastily; to cause to disappear; hide.

In other words, run like crazy!

Personal Application

With so many points that could be discussed, let's really focus on a person's "frame of mind." Philippians 4:8 defines what our mind-set should be. Scripture does not record whether or not Joseph tried to plead his innocence, nor does God's Word record Joseph going into a deep depression because of the rotten hand he was dealt. Throughout the rest of Genesis, Joseph demonstrated a proper perspective during all of his trials and tribulations.

Much of the Scripture demands that whatever appalling circumstance we find ourselves in, whether it was by our own doing or not, we must not dwell on the negative. Expend your mental energy on God!

Genesis 42:9

Then he remembered his dreams about them and said to them, "You are spies! You have come to see where our land is unprotected." (NIV)

The Lie

The famine had come and its severity was so great that Joseph had spent the previous seven years preparing Egypt for this massive event. Though Scripture does not say, it appears that the famine affected other countries as well, forcing people to come to Joseph for food. Jacob, Joseph's father, sent his sons—except Benjamin—to Egypt for food. When they arrived in the land, they had to meet Joseph. Joseph had become second in command in all of Egypt. When Joseph's brothers met him, they bowed down to him as a sign of respect. Joseph recognized his family, but they did not recognize him. Joseph also remembered the dreams he had about them.

Scripture records that Joseph spoke harshly to them, and he went on to accuse his brothers of being spies. The brothers tried to assure him they were not and told Joseph that they were sent by their father to buy food. Joseph, to test their words, demanded that they go and get Benjamin. To ensure their return, he kept Simeon.

Word Study

Dreams: H2472 [chalowm, or (shortened), chalom /khal·ome/]

To dream ordinary or to dream with a prophetic meaning.

A series of thoughts, images, or emotions occurring during sleep.

A visionary creation of the imagination.

Personal Application

Joseph accused his brothers four times for being spies (verses 9, 12, 14, and 16). Joseph was testing his brothers to see whether or not Benjamin was still alive. Because of what happened to Joseph, he did not believe his brothers' words. Because God did not intervene, neither for Joseph's brothers nor for the false accusations, we are left to wonder why. Even though this is prior to the Ten Commandments, it seems there would be a better way to test someone's words other than lying to them, especially because Joseph had experienced being falsely accused himself. In the end, it all works out according to all that God had preordained; nonetheless, Joseph lied.

- Is it right to lie to someone to test them?

- Even though Joseph lied and accused them of being spies, God did not intervene for the brothers of Joseph. Why?

- Why did Joseph keep Simeon and not Reuben? (Hint: see Genesis 37:21-31 again.)

- What are some proper ways to test someone's words to see if in fact they are true?

- What were the consequences, if any, of the lie?

Suggested
Reading:

Gen. 16:1-16

Genesis 42:11

"We are all sons of one man. We are honest men. Your servants have never been spies." (ESV)

The Lie

This verse is a continuation from the previous study. Here, Joseph's brothers were explaining to him why they had come to Egypt. During their discourse, they told Joseph about their father and other brother, Benjamin. Joseph, wanting to know whether Benjamin was still alive, accused them of being spies and ordered the brothers to go back to their home and bring back Benjamin. While speaking to Joseph, his brothers told him they were all "honest" men. At one point, in verse 13, they told Joseph that one of their brothers was no longer alive. This did not appear to be a lie on their part. Although it was obvious that Joseph was still alive, the brothers had come to actually believe Joseph was probably dead, because of the brutality that could come from being a slave. Not only that, so much time had passed, and they had not heard from Joseph. They might have convinced themselves of this to justify the continuing cover-up for their lie to their father, Jacob. It did not appear that any of Joseph's brothers confessed their sin to their father.

Personal Application

Defending your honor is one thing, but to defend your honor when you know you have none is another! Now, this is certainly not to say that a person without honor cannot grow to gain honor or even be honorable in some situations.

But when the majority of your life is self-focused, what is there to defend? Can you truly be known as a man or woman of honesty if at times you show none? Can you be a man or woman of honor, though at times you exhibit little?

Can you be known as a man or woman of compassion, though at times you ignore the weak and unfortunate? How can you defend your faith if you only believe some of God's Word and not all of it?

Word Study
Honest: H3653
[ken /kane/]

foot, base, place, office, estate

A noun from a theoretical root *knn* "to be firm, substantial." It denotes the physical base or foundation of something.

- Is it that easy to convince yourself of your own honesty? Explain.
- Are we that prideful that when a chance to confess comes, we choose to accept our own lies? Explain.
- Why is believing a lie much easier than believing the truth?
- Can a person without God show godliness, and can a person with God show godlessness?
- What do we need to do to distinguish ourselves from a godless world?
- What were the consequences, if any, of the lie?
- Do past sins identify you today?

Genesis 44:4-6

They had not gone far from the city when Joseph said to his steward, "Go after those men at once, and when you catch up with them, say to them, 'Why have you repaid good with evil? Isn't this the cup my master drinks from and also uses for divination? This is a wicked thing you have done.'" When he caught up with them, he repeated these words to them.   (NIV)

P.O.I.

Onychomancy is a form of divination by the fingernails. It was practiced by watching the reflection of the sun in the nails of a young boy. The future was judged by the shape of the figures which appeared on the surface.

The Lie

Joseph's brothers had returned from their homeland to Egypt and had brought with them their brother, Benjamin. Joseph then sat them down, in order of age, and had a meal with them. After the meal, Joseph commanded his steward to "fill the men's sacks with food…, and put each man's money in the mouth of his sack." (ESV) He also instructed his steward to put his silver cup in Benjamin's sack. Once his brothers left, he told his steward to chase after them and say the words in the above mentioned verse. When the steward told these words to Joseph's brothers, they gave him permission to search each bag. When the cup was found in the bag belonging to Benjamin, they tore off their clothes, which expressed great pain and torment in their hearts. They were all brought back to Joseph were Judah stepped forward and tried to protect Benjamin from becoming a slave, or, even worse, receiving the death penalty. Joseph was so moved, he could not contain himself any longer and confessed to his brothers his true identity.

Word Study
Divination: H5172
[nachash /naw·khash/]

to practice divination, divine, observe signs, learn by experience, diligently observe, practice fortunetelling, take as an omen

the art or practice that seeks to foresee or foretell future events or discover hidden knowledge usually by the interpretation of omens or by the aid of supernatural powers.

Personal Application

Once again, Joseph lied to test his brothers' loyalty to Benjamin. Joseph wanted to be sure that Benjamin was in no danger from his brothers, as well as seeing if his brothers' hearts had changed. This dramatic and heartfelt event lead to the disclosure of Joseph's identity. The act of finally revealing the truth led to the reuniting of Joseph's brothers and father. Do you see that it wasn't until the entire truth was confessed and revealed that God's purpose was finally understood? Truth should not be in partiality, and confession should not be just enough to appease yourself or someone else. Remember this: truth in whole means blessing in whole.

• Is the statement "partial forgiveness is no forgiveness" true?

• I have heard many Christians say that they believe in God but not in Satan. They believe in heaven and not in hell. They believe in God's grace but not in His judgment. Do these people hold the truth? Can these people claim to be Christians?

• What were the consequences, if any, of the lie?

Bibliography

Word Study: http://biblehub.com/tools.htm.

Point of Interest, page 7: http://www.answersingenesis.org/articles/2005/07/11/scopes-monkey-trial.

Point of Interest, page 9: http://www.disastercenter.com/crime/uscrime.htm.

Point of Interest, page 17: http://reocities.com/Athens/Forum/1611/sins22lies2.html.

Point of Interest, page 19: http://www.mayoclinic.com/health/legumes/NU00260.

Point of Interest, page 29: http://www.studylight.org/com/tpc/view.cgi?bk=0&ch=31.

Point of Interest, page 33: http://www.hmic.gov.uk/media/without-consent-20061231.pdf.

Point of Interest, page 37: http://health.nytimes.com/health/guides/symptoms/stress-and-anxiety/possible-complications.html.

Point of Interest, page 39: http://www.victoriana.com/VictorianPeriod/mourning.htm.

Point of Interest, page 41: http://www.makeitlouder.com/Decibel%20Level%20Chart.txt.

Point of Interest, page 47: http://www.thefreedictionary.com/onychomancy.

CPSIA information can be obtained at www.ICGtesting.com
Printed in the USA
LVOW02s0309240214

374914LV00010B/39/P